DAD
REMEMBERS

DAD REMEMBERS

Memories for My Child

CONCEIVED AND WRITTEN BY JUDITH LEVY

DESIGNED AND ILLUSTRATED BY JUDY PELIKAN

A WELCOME BOOK

STEWART, TABORI & CHANG

NEW YORK

Edited By Ellen Mendlow
Text copyright © 1993 by Judith Levy
Illustrations copyright © 1993 by Pelikan Inc.

Produced by Welcome Enterprises, Inc.
588 Broadway, New York, NY 10012

Published and distributed in the U.S. by
Stewart, Tabori & Chang,
a division of Harry N. Abrams, Inc.
115 West 18th Street, New York, NY 10011

ISBN 1-55670-595-6
Printed and bound in Singapore
7 9 10 8

Come walk the paths I've traveled,
And I'll stop along the way
To tell of how I grew up,
In a treasured yesterday.

With love for _____

From _____

Date _____

Table of Contents

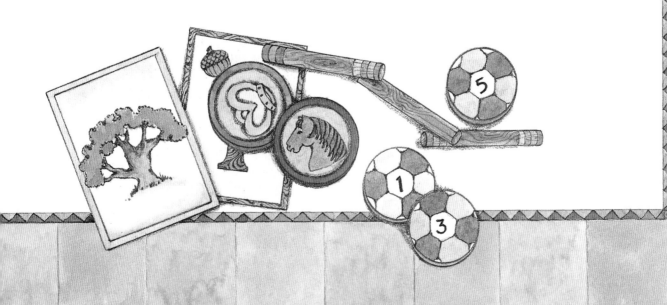

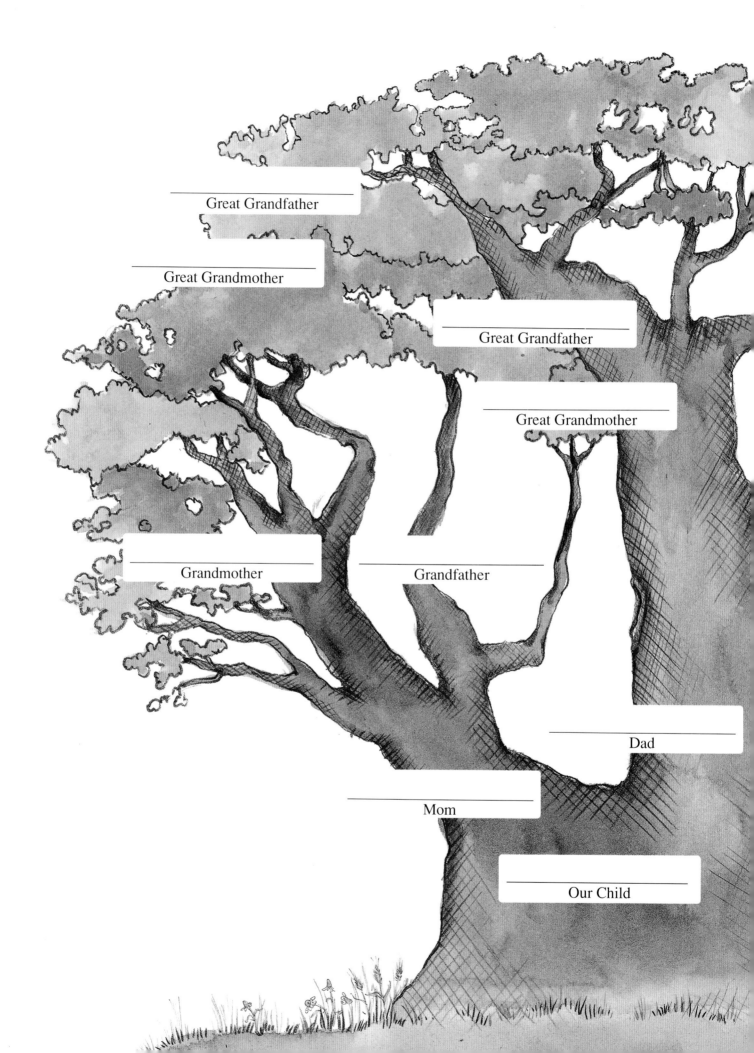

Great Grandfather

Great Grandmother

Great Grandfather

Great Grandmother

Grandmother

Grandfather

Dad

Mom

Our Child

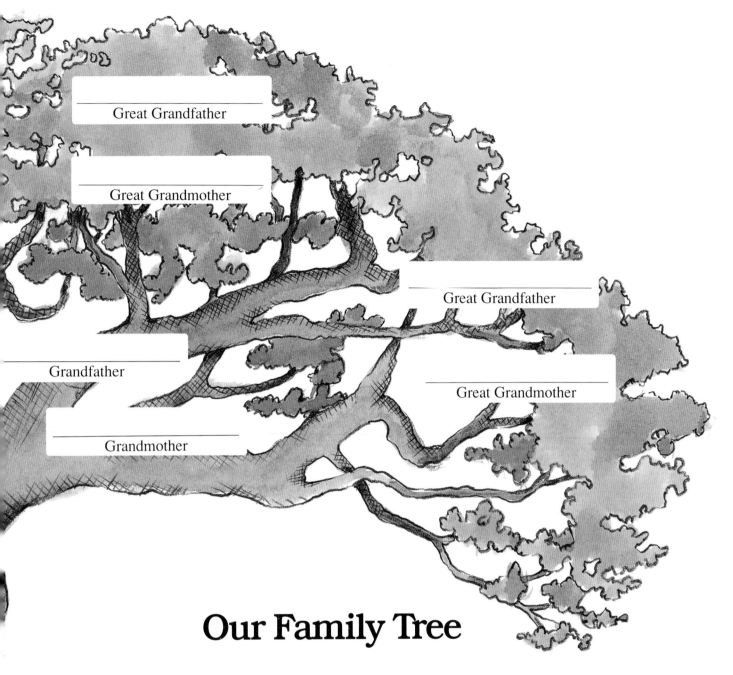

Great Grandfather

Great Grandmother

Great Grandfather

Grandfather

Great Grandmother

Grandmother

Our Family Tree

Welcome little one.
I know that you will see
You're loved and truly wanted
On our sturdy family tree.

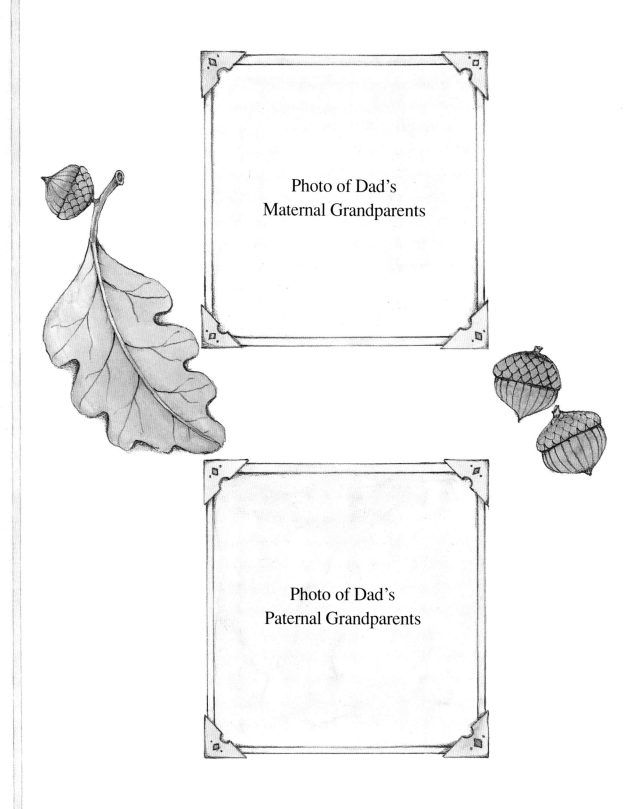

Photo of Dad's
Maternal Grandparents

Photo of Dad's
Paternal Grandparents

Our Grandparents

Our Grandparents were special,
Good people through and through.
You'll want to know about them,
Because they're part of you.

MY MOTHER'S PARENTS

My Grandfather's name _____

My Grandmother's name _____

Their heritage was _____

They made their home in _____

My Grandfather's occupation was _____

My Grandmother spent her days _____

What I treasured most about my Grandparents _____

_____

MY FATHER'S PARENTS

My Grandfather's name _____

My Grandmother's name _____

Their heritage was _____

They made their home in _____

My Grandfather's occupation was _____

My Grandmother spent her days _____

What I treasured most about my Grandparents _____

_____

Photo of Mom's
Maternal Grandparents

Photo of Mom's
Paternal Grandparents

MOM'S MOTHER'S PARENTS

Mom's Grandfather's name _____

Mom's Grandmother's name _____

Their heritage was _____

They made their home in _____

Mom's Grandfather's occupation was _____

Mom's Grandmother spent her days _____

What Mom treasured most about her Grandparents _____

_____

MOM'S FATHER'S PARENTS

Mom's Grandfather's name _____

Mom's Grandmother's name _____

Their heritage was _____

They made their home in _____

Mom's Grandfather's occupation was _____

Mom's Grandmother spent her days _____

What Mom treasured most about her Grandparents _____

_____

Photo of Dad's
Parents

My Parents

Oh, they were tough at times,
And at times they were sweet.
Yes, Mom and Dad were wonderful;
The word for them is "Neat."

My Father's name _____

My Mother's name _____

They met _____

They were married:

     When _____ Where _____

For their honeymoon they went to _____

Their first home was _____

My Dad's occupation _____

My Mother worked at _____

My parents encouraged me to _____

_____

They had strict rules about _____

_____

I think my Dad is the greatest because _____

_____

I think my Mom is the greatest because _____

_____

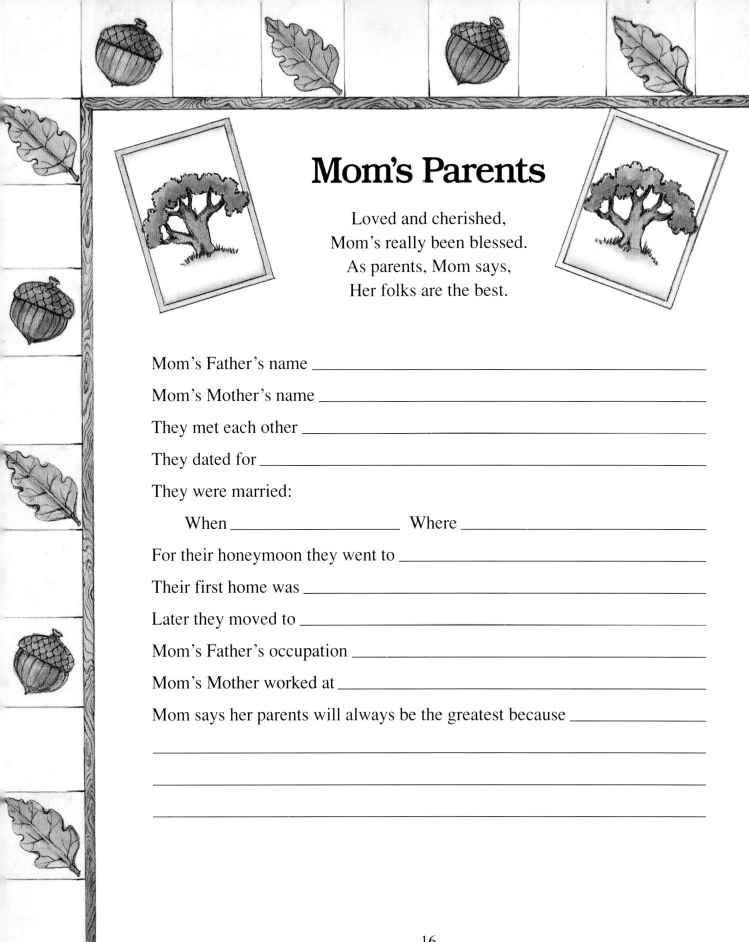

Mom's Parents

Loved and cherished,
Mom's really been blessed.
As parents, Mom says,
Her folks are the best.

Mom's Father's name _____

Mom's Mother's name _____

They met each other _____

They dated for _____

They were married:

　　　When _____ Where _____

For their honeymoon they went to _____

Their first home was _____

Later they moved to _____

Mom's Father's occupation _____

Mom's Mother worked at _____

Mom says her parents will always be the greatest because _____

_____

_____

_____

Photo of Mom's
Parents

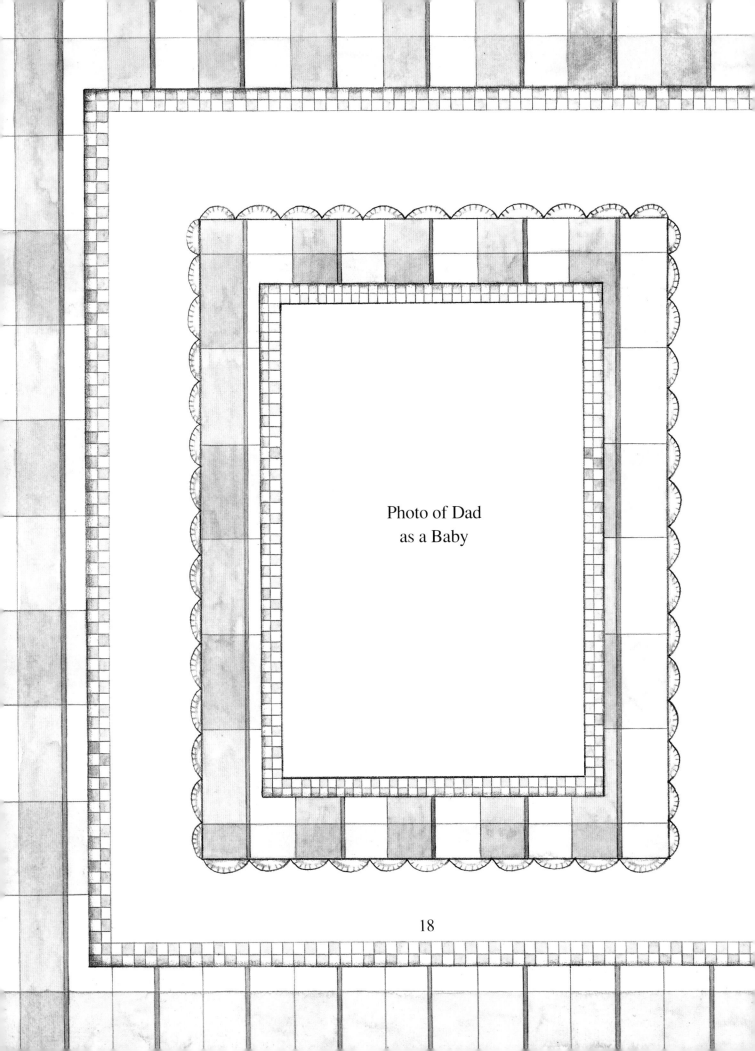

Photo of Dad
as a Baby

18

I Was Born

What can I tell you
About the day that I was born?
Just some simple facts;
You know I hate to blow my horn.

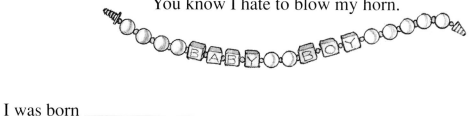

I was born _____

Where _____

I was named _____

My folks chose that name because _____

_____

I weighed _____

I was told I looked just like _____

Other members of my family are _____

_____

_____

_____

Additional thoughts _____

_____

_____

_____

_____

As a Youngster

I can't believe how much has changed.
The years just up and flew.
So, let me tell you how it was
When I was little, too.

My family lived _____

Our neighborhood was special because _____

_____

My room was _____

Around the house my jobs were _____

_____

When I was growing up I remember my parents were worried about _____

_____

As a student I _____

My ambition was _____

_____

My parents taught me to value _____

_____

For spending money I _____

_____

What I loved to do on weekends was _____

_____

KNIGHTS   Wildcats

I'll never forget the time _____

_____

_____

A scary experience was when _____

_____

I always laugh about the time _____

_____

_____

What I remember most about my boyhood years is _____

_____

_____

Photo of Dad
as a Boy

In my teens my best buddies were _____

Our favorite hangout was _____

The time I remember best of all was when _____

_____

When I grew up I wanted to be _____

My favorite sport to play was _____

A pet I loved was _____

My favorite television show was _____

My favorite book was _____

My favorite movie was _____

My favorite rock group was _____

A favorite slang expression was _____

Photo of Dad
as a Teenager

My Teenage Years

My folks were there for me,
Along the road from boy to man,
And it helped me to grow up,
To do the best I can.

A fashion craze of the time was _____

I used to wear my hair _____

I began shaving when I was _____

As a teenager I had a crush on _____

I started going out with girls when I was _____

I made my parents proud of me when _____

_____

I once got into trouble for _____

_____

The schools I attended were _____

_____

What I remember most about my teenage years is _____

_____

The best advice my Mom ever gave me was _____

_____

The best advice my Dad ever gave me was _____

_____

Wheels and Deals

To drive anywhere I wanted,
How free that would make me feel.
So I couldn't wait until the day
I got behind the wheel.

I was taught to drive by _____

The first car I drove was _____

My parents would let me use the family car when_____

_____

In those days a gallon of gas cost _____

The first car I owned was _____

I got the money for it by _____

_____

_____

The car I still dream of having is _____

_____

When I drive I'm always careful about _____

_____

_____

Some observations about driving _____

_____

_____

Photo of Dad
Behind the Wheel

The high school I graduated from was _____

Date _____

Then I _____

_____

A headline of the times was _____

My favorite political figure was _____

I felt that way because _____

_____

Photo of Dad
Around 20

A Fork in the Road

Lots of decisions,
More than just a few.
Go to school, take a job?
What's the right thing to do?

An event that made a difference in my life was _____

_____

My worries about the future were _____

_____

I felt good about _____

_____

My first job was _____

_____

What I remember most about that job is _____

_____

_____

I was always sorry I didn't _____

_____

_____

A good move I made was the time _____

_____

_____

Mom was born _____

Where _____

Her parents named her _____

That name was chosen because _____

_____

Other members of Mom's family are _____

_____

_____

Photo of Mom
as a Little Girl

Here's Mom!

Just a little history,
Of how it used to be
When Mom was small, when Mom grew tall,
And all about Mom and me.

Mom says the happiest memory of her childhood is _____

_____

_____

Schools Mom attended were _____

_____

Mom's ambition was _____

_____

Mom spent her school vacations _____

_____

Growing up, Mom says she was concerned about _____

_____

_____

Mom began dating at the age of _____

After high school Mom _____

_____

Mom's first job was _____

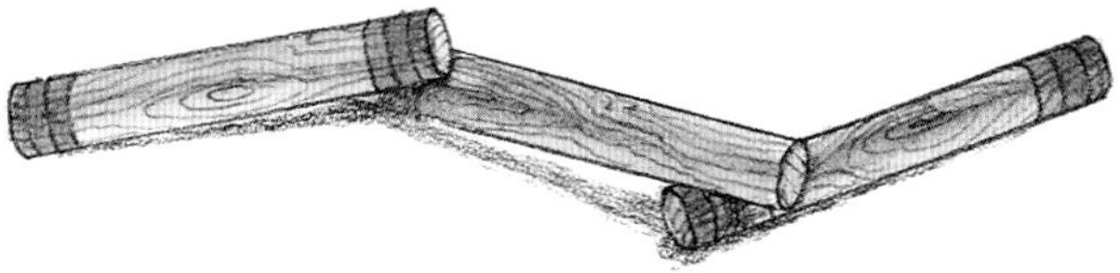

I met Mom:

Where _____

When _____

On our first date we _____

_____

I was attracted to Mom because _____

_____

_____

Mom said she liked me because _____

_____

_____

Our favorite place to go was _____

Our song was _____

We were sentimental about _____

We would talk about _____

We always loved to _____

_____

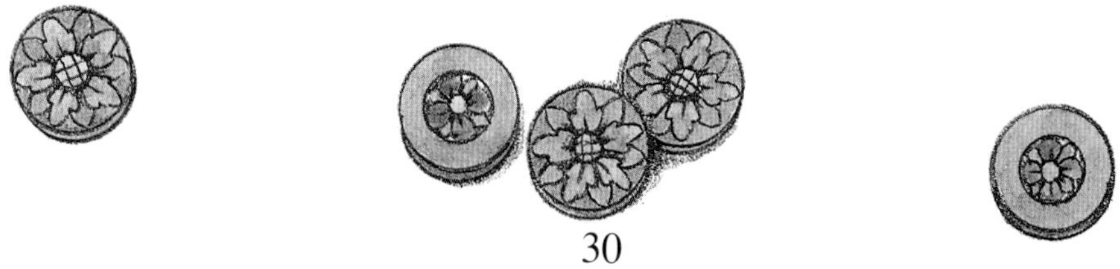

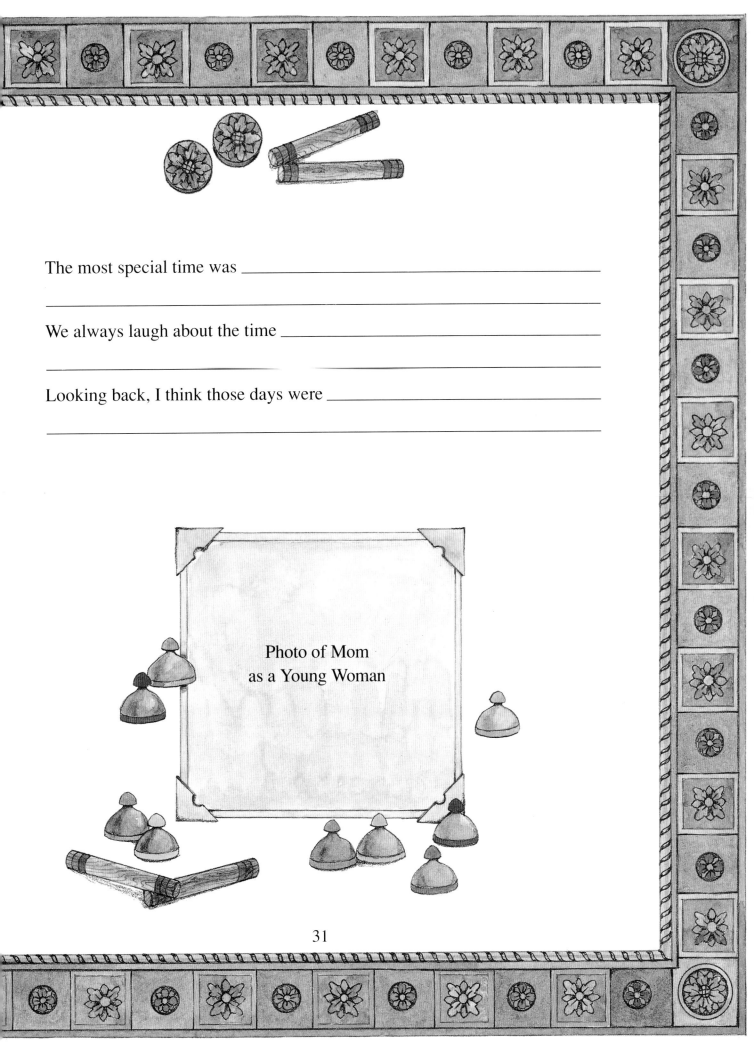

The most special time was _____

_____

We always laugh about the time _____

_____

Looking back, I think those days were _____

_____

Photo of Mom
as a Young Woman

Photo of
the Young Couple

Our Engagement

Comfortable and cozy,
We fit like hand in glove.
A partner to share my life,
Someone to share my love.

Mom and I dated for _____

My parents thought Mom was _____

_____

_____

Her parents thought I was _____

_____

_____

I knew she was the one for me because _____

_____

When I proposed to Mom, I said _____

_____

_____

And Mom said _____

_____

_____

We became engaged on _____

I gave Mom a gift of _____

Our Wedding Picture

Tying the Knot

The moment was powerful,
Filled with love and pride.
A solemn promise to cherish
My woman, my bride.

Mom and I were married:

Date _____ Time _____

Place _____

I wore _____

I remember Mom looked _____

_____

My best man was _____

Mom's maid of honor was _____

We celebrated our wedding by _____

_____

What I remember most about our wedding day is _____

_____

The gift I remember best was _____

After we were married we honeymooned at _____

_____

Special thoughts _____

_____

_____

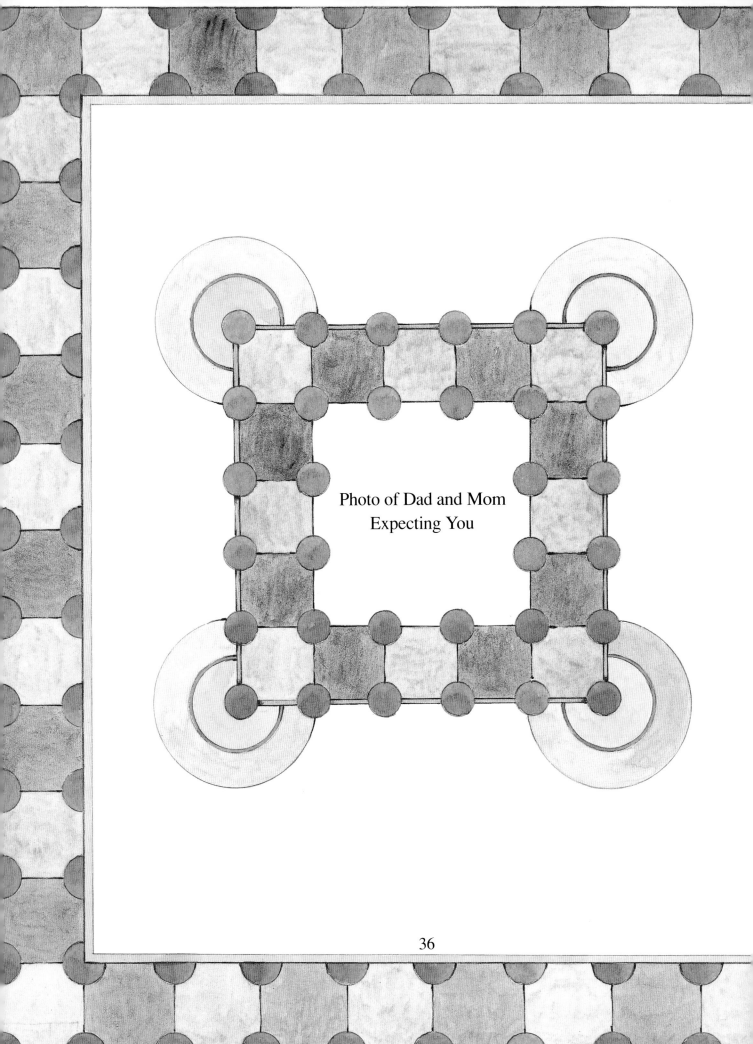

Photo of Dad and Mom
Expecting You

In the Beginning

Was she or wasn't she?
We had to know more,
So off to the doctor
To find out for sure.

Our doctor was _____

We definitely knew Mom was pregnant when _____

_____

Mom's reaction was _____

_____

I felt _____

_____

_____

I was concerned about _____

_____

The first people we told were _____

_____

Their reaction was _____

_____

Plans Mom and I made were _____

_____

_____

Waiting for You

Tried to learn all I could
While waiting months for you.
I wanted to be part of everything,
'Cause I was expecting, too!

I tried to help Mom by _____

_____

To prepare for you we _____

_____

When I first felt you move I _____

_____

What we learned about you before you were born was _____

_____

We had Mom's bag packed and ready by _____

_____

To get to the hospital on time, we practiced _____

_____

Whether you turned out to be a boy or a girl, my feelings were _____

_____

This pregnancy was a special time in our lives because _____

_____

_____

A Labor of Love

Packed and ready,
Today's the day.
Off to the hospital,
You're on your way.

The day you were born started out this way: _____

_____

_____

We first knew Mom was going into labor when _____

_____

During Mom's labor I was _____

_____

I first saw you when _____

I thought you looked _____

I'll always remember that moment because _____

_____

_____

Names we considered were _____

_____

What I'll remember most about the day you were born is _____

_____

_____

My Child

It's hard to express
The feelings I had.
'Cause you were a miracle,
And I was your Dad.

You were born on _____

Time _____ Place _____

Delivered by _____

Weight _____ Length _____

Hair color _____ Eye color _____

We named you _____

That name was chosen because _____

_____

A pet name I had for you was _____

Mom's first reaction was _____

_____

My reaction was _____

_____

_____

The first people I called were _____

_____

Everyone said you looked just like _____

A newspaper headline that day was _____

_____

As far as going to work was concerned I _____

_____

I loved you right away because _____

_____

_____

_____

Photo of You
as a Newborn
Baby

Changes

You're walking, you're talking,
You're growing up so fast.
I'd love to hold the clock back,
And make these moments last.

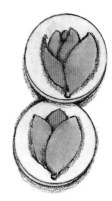

I could tell you recognized me when _____

_____

I felt ten feet tall when you first said _____

I got such a kick out of you the time _____

_____

I laughed so hard the time you _____

_____

_____

I never could convince you to eat _____

_____

When I put you to sleep I would always _____

_____

If you cried, my best method for comforting you was to _____

_____

I knew there was a deep bond between us because _____

_____

_____

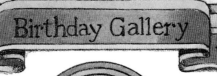

Birthday Gallery

Pictures, pictures, pictures,
I need quite a few
For this gallery of love
Filled with memories of you.

Photo of You
at Age One

What I remember most about this year is _____

_____

_____

_____

_____

2

Photo of You
at Age Two

What I remember most about this year is _____

_____

_____

_____

_____

3

Photo of You
at Age Three

What I remember most about this year is _____

_____

_____

_____

_____

4

Photo of You
at Age Four

What I remember most about this year is _____

_____

_____

_____

_____

5

Photo of You
at Age Five

What I remember most about this year is _____

_____

_____

_____

_____

47

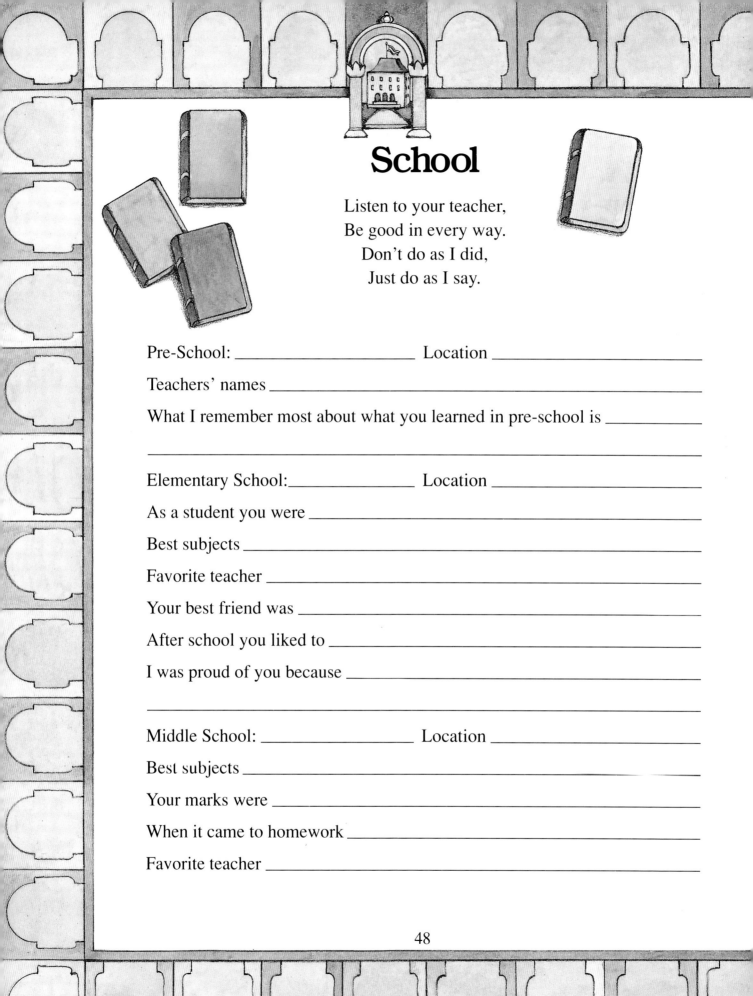

School

Listen to your teacher,
Be good in every way.
Don't do as I did,
Just do as I say.

Pre-School: _____ Location _____

Teachers' names _____

What I remember most about what you learned in pre-school is _____

_____

Elementary School:_____ Location _____

As a student you were _____

Best subjects _____

Favorite teacher _____

Your best friend was _____

After school you liked to _____

I was proud of you because _____

_____

Middle School: _____ Location _____

Best subjects _____

Your marks were _____

When it came to homework _____

Favorite teacher _____

Your best friend was _____

After school you liked to _____

I was proud of you because _____

_____

High School: _____ Location _____

Best subjects _____

Favorite teacher _____

Your best friend was _____

After school you liked to _____

One of the best times in high school was _____

_____

You graduated on _____

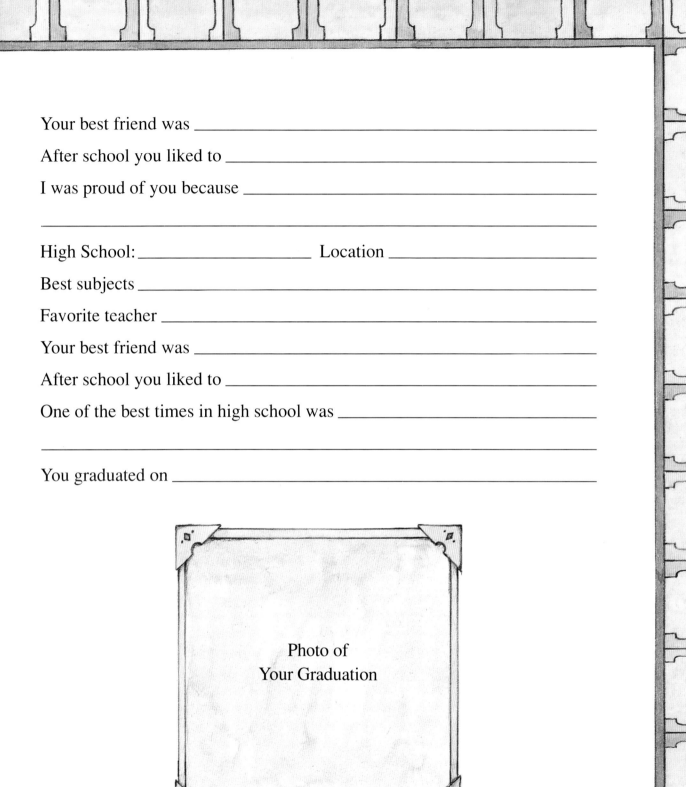

Photo of
Your Graduation

Our Times

Sometimes it's very special
For the two of us to see,
What mischief we can get into
Alone, just you and me.

We had such a good time the day we went to _____

_____

I'll never forget the trip we took to _____

_____

I had to convince you to _____

_____

_____

A special trip I still want to take with you is to _____

_____

It was special seeing things through your eyes when we travelled to ____

_____

I treasure our special times together because it gives me a chance to ____

_____

_____

I felt very close to you when _____

_____

_____

Holidays with You

Photo

When _____

Where _____

Who was there _____

Photo

When _____

Where _____

Who was there _____

Photo of
Family Member

Name _____

Relationship _____

Date _____

Photo of
Family Member

Name _____

Relationship _____

Date _____

Our Family

They love you very much.
They're people to remember.
Stepping up to take a bow,
This wonderful family member.

Photo of
Family Member

Name _____

Relationship _____

Date _____

Photo of
Family Member

Name _____

Relationship _____

Date _____

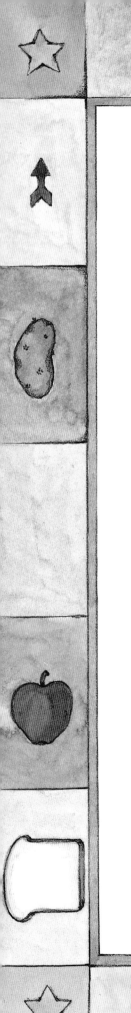

Photo of
Dad Cooking

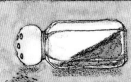

Let's Eat!

Alone in the kitchen
I can rustle up some grub.
But when it comes to clean-up,
I hate to clean and scrub.

My specialty is _____

Ingredients and Directions: _____

_____

_____

_____

_____

_____

My all-time favorite meal is _____

When it comes to carving a turkey I _____

_____

My favorite fast food is _____

When I raid the fridge I like to find _____

_____

A food we both love is _____

I'll always remember the time when _____

_____

_____

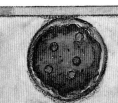

Sports!

Some Dads like baseball, football,
Golf, hockey, tennis, and more.
Well, let me tell you all about
The sports I'm cheering for.

I still love to play _____

My level of ability could be called _____

My favorite sport to watch is _____

My all-time favorite athlete is _____

My all-time favorite team is _____

My all-time dream match-up would be between _____

_____

_____

I'll never forget the time _____

_____

_____

I'd like to teach you _____

_____

_____

We had the most fun together playing _____

_____

_____

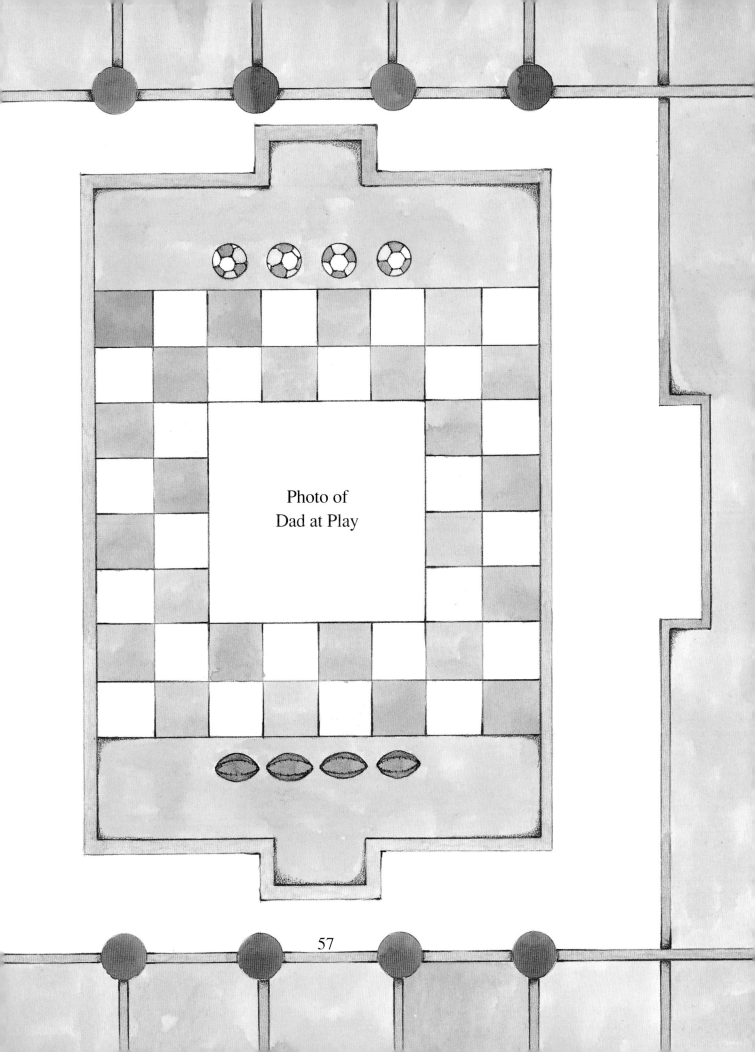

Photo of
Dad at Play

Photo of You
on Your Special Day

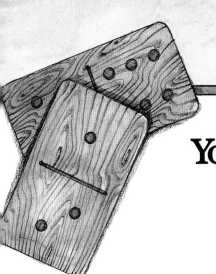
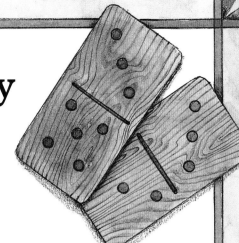

Your Special Day

I wish I could tell you
How proud I am of you.
So just let me say
How very much I love you.

This day was very special because _____
_____
_____

The preparations we made were _____
_____
_____

People who attended were _____
_____
_____

I was so proud of you this day because _____
_____
_____

What I'll remember most about this day is _____
_____
_____

You'll always be special to me because _____
_____

Go For It!

When you find a mountain,
See what's on the other side.
Take a risk, take a chance,
Be glad you really tried.

The best way to learn is to _____

_____

A risk I took that worked out was the time _____

_____

A risk that failed was when _____

_____

I learned not to _____

If you make a mistake, the best thing to do is _____

_____

When it comes to lending and borrowing money, my advice is _____

_____

If you go into a deal with someone, my advice is _____

_____

Things will generally work out best if you _____

_____

I trust your instincts because _____

_____

My Feelings

The feelings I have inside
I don't let many people see.
But I want you to know forever
What means a lot to me.

My deepest values are _____
_____
_____

My religious beliefs are _____
_____
_____

A code I've always lived by is _____
_____
_____

I believe in always doing _____
_____
_____

As a friend I try to be _____
_____

I think it's important for a person to _____
_____
_____

Men I admire _____

_____

Women I admire _____

_____

I know I can count on you to _____

_____

I've always been glad I'm your father because _____

_____

_____

People who influenced me the most were _____

_____

They made a difference in my life because _____

_____

_____

My pet peeve is _____

_____

I have always regretted I didn't _____

_____

Everyone said I shouldn't, but I was glad I _____

_____

I was always proud of the time I _____

_____

Treasures

Precious little treasures,
I've saved quite a few.
Remembrances of the past,
Especially for you.

Report card, diploma, invitation, announcement,
business card, or any memento of the past

The Future

When the years have passed
And you're a parent, too,
I wish you all the happiness
That I've had loving you.

My wish for your future is _____

_____

_____

I tried to be the best Dad I know how, and if there's one thing I'd like

you to remember, it's that _____

_____

_____

Recent Photo
of Dad